I0761346

Between Curses ¦ Bainne Géar

Colette Nic Aodha

Between Curses ¦ Bainne Géar

ISBN 10: 1–903631–86–6
ISBN 13: 978–1–903631–86–7

Foilsithe ag Arlen House ¦ First published in October 2006 by

Arlen House
PO Box 222
Galway
Phone/Fax: 00 353 86 8207617
Email: arlenhouse@gmail.com

Distributed in North America by Syracuse University Press

Syracuse University Press
621 Skytop Road, Suite 110
Syracuse, NY 13244–5290
Phone: 315–443–5534/Fax: 315–443–5545
Email: supress@syr.edu

Clochur ¦ Typesetting: Arlen House
Priontáil ¦ Printing: Betaprint

Tugann Bord na Leabhar Gaeilge tacaíocht airgid do Arlen House

CONTENTS ¦ CLÁR

EARTH ¦ DÚLRA

JOURNEY ¦ AISTEAR

MEMORIES ¦ CUIMHNÍ

ART ¦ EALAÍN

The poems that follow in this dual language collection are neither fact nor fiction, but the product of this writer's imagination. Whether I write in Irish or English is determined by a number of factors, not least being association of place or person.

Is as Breac-Ghaeltacht mé agus dá bhrí sin ní raibh an Ghaeilge agam ó dhúchas. Mhothaigh mé í thart timpeall orm, áfach, agus ba í an teanga ba ghaire dom chroí í cé nach raibh sí á labhairt agam.

Bhíodh go leor Gaeilge á múineadh sa scoil áitiúil agus d'fhoghlaim mé níos mó, ar bhealach, sa bhunscoil ná a d'fhoghlaim mé as sin amach. Ní hé nach raibh deis foghlama san ollscoil ach ag an aois sin bhínn níos minicí amuigh le mo chuid cairde nuair ba chóir dom a bheith ag léachtaí nó ag staidéar. Ach is leis na cairde sin a labhair mé Gaeilge.

D'fhás mo ghean don teanga agus mhéadaigh mo líon cairde. Ó d'fhágas an ollscoil bhínn ag plé leis an nGaeilge i slí amháin nó i slí eile. An chéad uair riamh a leagas peann ar pár bhínn ag scríobh i nGaeilge agus i mBéarla. Ba mhinic a rinne mé machnamh ar cén chaoi ar roghnaigh mé cén teanga inar scríobh mé dánta áirithe, cé nár rud é a rabhas consiasach faoi agus mé á scríobh.

Imagination is a facet of everyday existence. Some see it as the way we perceive the world; the way we add to, subtract from or reorganise reality. A friend of mine referred to this recently as *faction,* what we as writers tap into, not fact merely, not exactly fiction either, but rather a slice of both with free reign given to imagination.

I was delighted to recently discover that there is a scientific term for this, what some may perceive as madness, this strange affliction that forces some of us to become writers. This term, aesthetic realism, is the reorganisation of reality in our minds and it always has a purpose. We put part of ourselves into every situation that we deal with. The way we alter reality can be useful or harmful, the moulding of the world as we see it into beautiful shapes which please us and others has an artistic purpose. But when we alter facts in a way that is harmful, we encounter ugliness, cruelty and an element of mental instability. This is the other side of the coin of imagination that none of us would like to explore. Art in general and writing in particular is a form of escapism, an exercise in imagination. Writers shape their own worlds. What I am actually doing bears no resemblance to reality of place, people or other.

I recall after a reading in London in the late nineties, my cousin, who always spent her school holidays with us in Mayo, approached me afterwards and laughed at the fact that the countryside and life as I had described it in the poems about our childhood were not as she remembered. Unless you are a biographer most writers' work involves delving anxiously into the world of the imagination. Reality only acts as a springboard for the creative process and inspiration is manipulated in different ways.

Bíonn baint ag áiteanna éagsúla agus daoine éagsúla im shaol leis an mBéarla nó leis an nGaeilge, cinnte, ach i gcás na Gaeilge sílim go bhfuil níos mó i gceist. Ní fheadar dá dtuigfeadh gach duine an Ghaeilge an mbeinn ag scríobh dánta áirithe ar chor ar bith?

Ar bhealach caithfidh mé a admháil corruair nuair a scríobhaim i nGaeilge bíonn sé ar nós go mbím ag tógáil balla thart timpeall orm, balla nach mbeadh mórán in ann a leagan. An balla seo do mo chosaint agus mé ag baint tairbhe as dánta a chumadh agus an racht a ligint amach.

Féachaim ar léarscáil m'óige agus is ansin a fheicim an Béarla briste a labhair mé agus mé ag fás aníos. Formhór de na focail a bhí sa bhfoclóir againn, focail Ghaeilge a bhí iontu. Aisteach go leor bhí orm mo bhaile dúchais a fhágáil agus dul go cathair na Gaillimhe chun mo theanga dhúchais a labhairt. Ní dhéanfaidh mé dearmad go deo ar an gcéad uair a bhí mé ag brionglóidigh as Gaeilge. Ar an gCeathrú Rua a bhí mé agus thuig mé ansin go raibh sí agam idir chorp agus anam.

Colette Nic Aodha

Gaillimh, 2006

Nollaig Mac Congáil
Alan Hayes
Cathal Ó Searcaigh
Pádraig Ó Snodaigh
Fidelma Sheridan and family
Jane O'Hanlon, Joe Woods
Bridget, Kerim and Dara Yildiz
Oldtown Design
The staff at Syracuse University Press

Poems in this collection were previously published in:

Poetry Ireland Review
The Irish Pages
Virtual Writer
Words on the Web
Writing in the West
Cyphers
Black Mountain Review
The Cork Literary Review
Comhar
Feasta
Lá
An Guth
Go Nuige Seo
Divas: A Sense of Place (editor, Nuala Ní Chonchúir)

Body Corp

UNEASY DISTANCE

I'd love to invent a yardstick
that would readily measure
your distance,

a scale has yet to be invented
that counts in centimetres
how near or far you wish to be,

how often to touch, speak, text, kiss.
I tried out a calculus
but its digits didn't suit,

when the time wasn't right
you withdrew,
re-emerged in a rainbow

only to fade shortly after,
ever since then nothing,
zero, nought.

Cúpla Céad Míle

Súile gorma orm
m'aghaidh lasta
m'aigne iata

tarlaíonn sé
gach tráthnóna
i gciúnas

an tseomra ranga
do shúile gorma orm
m'aghaidh lasta

cromtha
tú cúpla céad míle uaim
de ghnáth.

Wisdom

You are wise when you do not answer,
I envy your wisdom,
all I have is my foolishness,

the memory of your handsome face,
kiss, longing to hold you in my arms,
please forgive me this.

Ceist

Nuair a fhéachaim sa scáthán ar maidin
corruair labhraíonn sé ar ais chugam
níl dóthain ama agat smideadh a chur ort,
tú faoi bhrú ama

"déan rud éigin le do chuid gruaige
í ar fud na háite, gan srian, gan smacht".
Ní haon ionadh nach maith liom
breathnú isteach rómhinic,

bíonn sé deacair orm
comhairle ionraic a ghlacadh.
ní chuireann sé isteach ná amach orm
cén chuma a bhíonn orm

nuair a deir sé liom:
breathnaigh ort féin, tú ag obair
le sé bliana déag
is tú gan a bheith buan go fóill,

céard tá ort nach bhféadfá post ceart a fháil?
ní hé nach bhfuil tú cáilithe, tá,
bhuel, céard tá le rá agat?
Bhuel, céard tá le rá?

Nerves, excitement,
anticipation I don't understand,
another handsome man,
his pocket wears a wedding ring.

Just the right height,
intelligent words,
smiles, jokes,
no exchange of numbers,

no future plans.
Face well moisturised,
no beard rash,
warmth of shared scent of skin

remains until the days shorten,
night extends.
Who pities the shallowness
of lives lived?

Tost

Tá sé níos réadúla an ciúnas seo
ba mhian liom scairteadh os ard
ach ní fhéadfainn,

fonn orm dreapadh suas an sliabh
atá taobh thiar díom
agus liú in airde mo ghutha.

Bíonn sé deacair srian a chur
ar mo chuid focal,
ar fhocail amháin a mhairim.

Braithim tuiscint eadrainn,
tuiscint a leáfadh dá n-osclóinn mo bhéal.
Cé nach bhfuil sé de chumas ionam

do chuid smaointí a léamh
thug mé faoi deara rabhadh gan focal
a d'eisigh tú.

ZODIAC

Today I look into the houses of the moon
High Priestess of Babylon points out my route,

Girdle of Ishtar doesn't give a green light
to my expectation of affairs on the twenty ninth

I pass through seven gateways, feel my descent,
each worldly attachment discarded

wrap myself in seven veils,
inhale the scent of cedar incense.

Faoi Ghlas

Doras dúnta
Gach áit a gcasaim
Tusa romham
á chur faoi ghlas.

D'oscail mé arís é
ag fiafraí díot
cén treo?
Bláthanna in áit mo shúl.

Shiúil mé ar aghaidh
Ag ceapadh gur ar oscailt
a bhí sé
is tú á dhúnadh arís.

Bhí brionglóid agam,
an doras ar oscailt,
ach é ceangailte go docht.
Ar maidin mé ar shiúl

Náire orm
gur thug éinne faoi deara
m'aghaidh scriosta,
baracáid in áit do dhorais.

Along The Line Of Your Palm

Sea breeze scurrying from the strand
escapes in your window,

winds its way to your chamber,
seeking out where your pen touched paper,

unfurls itself among your books,
brushing each leaf, invisible, it slips

between your fingers,
along the line of your palm,

up your arm, curls your shoulder,
licks your neck, breezes your cheek,

blows your candle out.
No one notices ... no one.

Scáth na maidine ag ardú beagáinín,
fuinneog na traenach mar shleaspholl im shaol,
cos nocht i riteoga *fishnet* é an solas
ag stealladh trí phiolón.

D'fhág do phóg dheireanach
im ghlóthach mé. Díslí aisteacha
iad na bearta sadhlais dúchlúdaithe
le *x*anna bána orthu.

Na cluichí a imrítear!

Réamhtheagmháil a bheadh
in aon ghlaoch fóin uaim.
Dalladh dubh a bhí ann
nuair a leag tú lámh orm.

Aghaidh dhúnárasach orm anois
Is gan ar intinn agam
iomlán mo chártaí
a chur amach ar mo bhois.

An iomarca cuireataí hairt
faighte agam go dtí seo.

Statues

I wish we were smooth white marble
our naked bodies wrapped around each other
nothing visible other than our coolness,

a portion of granite, enough
to hold us, carefully folded
into one another, bodies inseparable ivy.

Although colourless and made of a class
of a rock the warmth of our kiss-embrace
reverberates.

In reality we are the opposite to rock,
just once you locked your lips with mine.

Feoite

Caithim an lá ag cuartú brí led thost,
ó thráth go chéile déanaim staidéar ar an gcoimhneas
idir na sracfhéachaintí nár sheol tú ar ais.
Meáim na focail nár dúradh,

léim ar na ríomphoist nár seoladh,
déanaim iarracht cothromú a fháil
idir na nithe réalaíocha agus na cinn nach bhfuil.
D'fhás an féithleann atá ar an mbord

ón talamh clochach os comhair do thí,
eitlím go neamh faoi racht seoil
is mé ag féachaint orthu.
Go mbaineann tú an teaspach díom

leis an tsúil nach dtugann tú orm,
níl mórán de do chuid agam le coinneáil
ach féithleann ag feo
is cúpla líne nár scríobh tú chugam.

Love is many things but patience isn't one of them.
This I found out to my cost the last time I sported
my heart pinned to my stripy blouse. I thought
each atrium and ventricle just loosely tacked in place.

Days later I realised that they had been machine stitched,
tried vainly with a blade to unpick the threads.
You certainly have the measure of me with your
single email after a wait of seven days, seven

mornings, seven nights. In the meantime I had bled
each place I went, car, work, home, all over the table
in a fancy restaurant. Someone tried to insert
an intravenous line that would reach my stomach,

but it resisted all sustenance.
Some gentle presence sang a sweet song
into my ear, nothing so severe
as seven days of heart waiting.

Socrú

Tá mo lámha gan mhaith
mo chosa gan fuinneamh
mo cholainn gan neart

níl fuil ag rith trí m'fhéitheoga
ní thig lem scamhóga
breith ar m'anáil

a bhfuil laistigh ar stailc
a bhfuil lasmuigh gan neart
chuile shórt folamh

ach mo chloigeann,
é plúchta le smaointí amaideacha
íomhánna seafóideacha

focail gan bhrí
brí gan focail
céard a tharlódh dá …

cén fáth nár …
tosaíonn na focail ag bruíon lena chéile
sciobann na hainmfhocail na briathra

téann na haidiachtaí i bhfolach
ní féidir míniú a fháil áit ar bith
mo chorp sínte ar leaba

ní liomsa mo chorp
céard a thógfadh sé chun brí a aimsiú arís
tá a fhios agam go bhfuil socrú simplí

ar an scéal casta seo
ní thógfadh sé ach glaoch gutháin
uait.

Chemical Warfare

White Phosphorus
settled on my skin,
flesh all aflame.

No amount of dousing
could extinguish your touch.
Epidermis melted,

can't hold eye contact,
stupid blushes,
head bowed towards floorboards,

a crouched position
hides this scorched heart.

Cheal Tréimhsí Gréine

Scamall dorcha ag luí ar mo chloigeann
dhún sé mo shúile
gach rud dubh agus gruama.

D'oscail an scamall mo bhéal,
d'ith mé na nóiméid, na huaireanta, na seachtainí,
lean mo ghruaim ar aghaidh.

Cuireadh comhairle orm
dul i ngleic leis
meáchan a chailliúint.

Thosaigh mé ag siúl -
chuaigh an scamall in éag
ar ball chonaic mé an ghrian ag teacht tríd.

Inbox

Your name in capitals
the only one I keep
others rarely survive the day
in my inbox

your Christmas wish
endures until the harsh wind of March
sounds in nearby trees,
my electronic one-sided diary

opening up, spilling its words
into the palm of my hand,
my clenched fist,
text, release,

the dagger of your voice
uses my heart as a sheath.

Luas na Gaoithe

Turas eile
liom féin
seanfhear ina shuan
trasna uaim.

Íomhánna daite
faram
amach an fhuinneog
gach sórt ag rith

ar luas na gaoithe
n'fheadar an bhfuil
siad ag dul i dtreo rud éigin
nó a mhalairt.

An bhfuilim féin
ag brostú i do threo
nó ag cúlú
ón rud atá romham?

FLY-FISHING

Soft as an insect's wing on water
your line flutters,
flies wear a clever disguise,
home-made copper wire coils

around plumes of varied hue.
My hands too clumsy to trace
any such delicacies.
Your nimble fingers, keen intellect

trawls through my responses
as you set your bait,
wait for the bite,
time is on your side.

TINTE BEALTAINE

Triailim an scéal a léamh
sna réaltaí, sa spéir.

Bealtaine ag teacht
go gairid, cén bhaint

atá ag an ngealach
le pé rud

a thitfidh amach. Smaoiním
ar na féilte eile

Imbolg, Samhain, Lúnasa.
Ach tusa, Bealtaine, féile tine,

las tine ina chroí
faigh teas an tsamhraidh

agus déan grá as, domsa, uaidh.
Nach ionann tine agus grá, paisean,

teastaíonn uaim tine a lasadh lasmuigh
agus damhsa timpeall uirthi.

Your *boudoir* of music
was a feather eiderdown
after a night of cabaret,

eyes widened at the sight,
wooden layers held parallelograms,
between their covers

my life in music.
As the needle hit each disc
I was in college, hippy chick,

drinking or crying, Tom Waits,
heartbreak, Springsteen,
talking of Talking Heads,

in JFK Stadium Philadelphia
swaying to Dylan and The Grateful Dead,
losing it all to *A Whiter Shade Of Pale,*

yearning for Kiss,
alcohol to dilute awkwardness.
I am eighteen again,

after your spectrum of song
everything is music.

Gealach Dhorcha

Súil agam nach mbeidh
gealach dhorcha amuigh anocht
súil agam go mbeidh tú ann romham

súil agam nach bhfuilimid ag druidim
chuig deireadh
súil agam nach mbeidh orm

tosú as an nua
súil agam nach mbeidh mé
croíbhriste agat arís.

A Ghealach Dhorcha, fan istigh anocht.

Still life

She sits at the table
in front of her is an empty bowl

a pink rose in a white vase
a glass half full

uneaten bread
triangles of napkins

a jug of water
opposite is a vacant chair

it rests snug against the table.
After expectation.

Gruaim Gan Ghrá

Ag siúl na sráide ar maidin sa dorchadas
cé go raibh an ghrian éirithe
ní raibh puinn solais ann.

Chuile áit faoi scamall dubh
de bharr na gealaí duibhe
a sheol tú chugam aréir.

Caithfidh mé dul i ngleic
leis an gcríoch
níl tada againn níos mó

ba chóir dom machnamh géar
a dhéanamh air, tagann deireadh
le gach ní, bíodh siad maith nó olc,

deireadh liom, deireadh leat,
deireadh linn, deireadh le grá
fiú, am éigin, deireadh le gruaim.

The Path

You wake me at five,
lakeside walk dawns,
thorns of what didn't transpire,
you were my pillow all night.

After breakfast I circled water,
plucked your first 'hello'
from the hedge, Honeysuckle,
walked towards your smile, Woodbine.

What a pleasant scent,
leaves of chatter, Heartsease,
with someone else, White Helleborine,
my cupped fist around stems.

You poured more wine, Rock Rose,
accidental touch, Meadowsweet.
Another sits near you,
my thoughts roamed, Rhododendron.

What if …? Star-Of-Bethlehem …
I watch my step, Birds-Foot,
if I asked you? Wild Clematis or Dog Rose?
I break an Elderflower from its branch,

dewy grass highlights my steps
but hides the path.
Flowers fall from my hands,
scattered arrangement.

Kali

Scríobh bandia ón Ind
d'ainm ar mo chroí
sé mhí ó shin.

Ar an séú lá dhéag
de mhí na Samhna
chuir tú mór-roinn eadrainn

bhí céiliúradh in onóir Kali.
Caitheann Kali creatlacha
ina slabhra timpeall a muiníl.

Fuair sí neart cnámh uaimse
ghoid sí mo chreatlach
chuile uair a chuir tú

chun báis mé led
dhíláithreachas, easpa teagmhála,
uair a cuireadh mo chorp faoin bhfód

tagadh Kali is gan aon
tsúil léi, itheadh sí mo chroí fuar
led ainm scríofa air

cuireadh sí mo chreatlach
timpeall uirthi ansin
ardaíodh sí a ceithre lámha

cuireadh sí ar ais ar talamh mé,
mo chreatlach fós uirthi,
d'ainm ar mo chroí

bíonn orm
dul tríd an gcroíbhriseadh
arís is arís is arís eile fós.

Sorcerer

He, who intoned,
not song or poems
but doom itself,

or so it seemed,
his words,
I can't erase.

They grip
with ivy intent,
not a vein escapes.

Ainmním gach dóchas atá agam
cuirim ar d'altóir iad
mar a chuirtí dhá bhuilín aráin

ar altóir Lúnasa. Feicim glas
agus oráiste gach áit,
maireann gach dóchas

toisc go tugann na dathanna geala beocht dóibh,
mé fós sínte ar d'altóir
las tine ar mo shon lasmuigh.

A Cold Hand Greets Me

I reach to the East
you are not there,
I reach to the West,

where you never would be.
I reach to the North
a cold hand greets me,

I reach to the South,
a warm breath,
not yours.

ULCHABHÁN

A Ulchabháin, lán le heolas na hoíche,
deirtear gur tusa Bloduewedd,

go raibh corp maighdine agat tráth,
go ndearnadh tú as bláthanna,

níor ghéill tú d'aon fhear.
Is ba mhian liom cogar id chluas -

An rachfá ar mo shonsa
chuig mo ghrá bán

m'ainm a rá os íseal leis na mílte uair
ionas go gcloisfidh a chroí é.

My muse divorced me recently,
yesterday I found a bright blue marker,
it looked handsome against a blank page.

The nib rounded words of its own accord.
Sinews that unite fingers and heart
felt severed. I rejoiced at the end result,

your *billet-doux*.

Athbheochan

Is fuil mhíosúil a sú
atá ag teacht go fras
nuair a roinnim an phomagránait

le scian ghéar
broinn scoilte in dhá leath
feicim an bheocht ag imeacht

bainim an craiceann di
agus fágaim é
ar leataobh

tá mo chraiceann féin leis
itheann na hanamacha
faoi thalamh mo thorthaí,

na pomagránaití uilig
ionas go dtiocfaidh siad ar ais,
is go mairfidh siad arís.

Voice

Clot of sweet cream on tongue tip
new feather pillow beneath your head
handful of sand from the beach
purple taffeta over-the-top dress

first touch of new skin
roll of wheels down a hill
earths most elusive nectar
as welcome as a mother's prayer.

Sa chéad cheathrú anois
mé chun tosú as an úrnua,
spriocanna, pleananna
a chur i gcrích
gach deis a thapú.

Faoin am a thiocfaidh
an dara ceathrú
mé faoi lánseol,
obair fhiúntach déanta agam,
tuilleadh dánta scríofa
go leor turas tugtha agam.

Sa tríú ceathrú
feicfidh mé chuile ní
le cabhair ó sholas na gealaí
beidh tuiscint agam dá bharr.

An cheathrú dheireaneach
iompóidh mé thart
agus tiocfaidh sé chun solais
níl sé tuillte agat
an grá seo atá agam duit.

Bratacha *Beckett* ar Foluain

I gcroílár na cathrach
tháinig mé chuig na háiteanna
inar chaitheamar am fadó
tháinig mé orthu de thimpiste,

gan fios an bhealaigh agam,
ar dtús
mé faoi bhratacha *Beckett 100*
chonaic go tobann an bhialann

inar itheamar an chéad oíche,
mhothaigh mé lán.
Trasna na sráide bhí an tábhairne
ina rabhamar nuair a scaramar

ón slua, thíos píosa bhí an caifé
mar a rabhamar an tráthnóna dár gcionn
tar éis oíche a chaitheamh le chéile
oíche agus tú i do luí taobh liom

craiceann le craiceann.
Aréir i gcroílár na cathrach
chuir mé an gúna orm
a chaith mé nuair a bhuail mé leat

an chéad uair, bláthanna ag fás air,
d'fhág mé an teach ósta
agus shiúil mé síos
go dtí na háiteanna

inar chaitheamar am
na háiteanna a bhí díreach
aimsithe agam arís
shuigh mé ar an suíochán

céanna, d'ól mé an deoch chéanna,
d'ith mé an bia céanna,
trasna uaim bhí cathaoir fholamh
crúiscín leathlán

rós dearg i mbláthchuach
dallóga síos
doras iata
coinnle dubha lasta.

Spiddal

Spiddal's fresh air swam up my nose
your coldness
a continuous shoreline
shrinking into shelled horizons

unmutual affection
a jellyfish between my toes
soft, spongy, golden
full of poison.

On tepid sand caked rock hard
we walked hand away from hand
in the cemetery
of our failed romance.

Bhíomar óg nuair a phósamar
lus na gréine curtha agat i bprócaí
gach áit thart orainn
ag titim as a chéile.

B'aoibhinn liom suí ar an mbalcóin
i dteas na gréine ag déanamh iontais
dár mbláthanna:
ba ghnách linn síolta a chur.

An t-earrach nó samhradh
A bhíodh ann i gcónaí
ní fhacamar aon gheimhreadh ná fómhar
ar feadh cúig bliana.

Nuair a tháinig athrú ar na séasúir
athrú suntasach a bhí ann;
th'éis fómhair ghearr amháin
bhí sé ina gheimhreadh feasta.

A Curse on Those who Harassed Me at Work

A curse on those who harassed me at work
on their next bite may they choke,
their every phone call be a hoax,
may they need an undertaker and a priest
before next midsummer feast,
may someone forget to pay Charon,
their flesh and blood be rat infested carrion.

May their every effort end in failure,
unreasonable, dysfunctional, uncouth harasser,
may their every cup fall from the dresser,
their every bicycle be without mud-splasher.
Each time they go for a stroll
may they end up eye-deep in a pot hole.

May each month see them up the duff,
their every golden thing turn to fluff,
oh! they who are full of poisonous stuff
may their ill gotten gains go up in a smoking puff.
The curse of poets on their head
for every malicious word they said.

When I think of the threats they uttered
I wish their offspring permanently scuttered,
each penny they earn that they may flutter,
and they unable to talk but stutter.
May every ill settle on their head
and they never rest easy in their bed
for my good name they stole
may they be eternally engulfed in a flaming black hole.

For all the sleepless nights they caused me
may they go completely crazy,
may their only visitor be a flea
and he to bring his extended family.
Be they bad minded, jealous, or malefactors
this poet never forgets her detractors.

A Curse on The Piper who Called The Tune

I know it wasn't much of a job
thirteen euro a night
no taxi home
but as a single mother on the dole

it kept the wolf from the door
bad cess to the piper who called the tune
that he may never hear
beetle around from year to year

that his hands seize up
fingers on pipe.
for each time he pounded the door
may he lose a clump of hair

for each complaint he made
may he grow another head
and I won't say where
that he turn to compost

before the year is past.

In Company on *Barr Chiaráin*

Life took on a different perspective
from the summit of *Barr Chiaráin,*
windmills scolded the air, their magnificent
white height couldn't but impress.

Bog cotton regrouped in swallow holes,
their wave almost a dare,
pretty pink blossoms assembled in different
orders, dark peat of wetlands,

brown peat of higher ground, bright peat
thinly stripped from the earth,
perfect lines reasserting themselves,
were their own art gallery.

Old school house on the left was the aristocrat,
it lorded over the landscape
that rolled down to Clew Bay.
One Nephin shelters the other,

shy and retiring Clare Island
barely making an appearance,
Croagh Patrick is its own church steeple,
Sunday morning, I felt blessed.

COSMIC LIFT

Even more pleasure in birdsong
you gave me dawn,
since you enveloped me in your arms
there hasn't been nightfall

or even dusk,
perennial sun
flowers plentiful
cut-grass perfume even sweeter,

sky free of cloud is making a two-way mirror with the sea.
I want to stop smoking, drink less, take exercise.
River current has eased to gentle ebb
waves turned ripples,

mountains, taller, glisten with colour,
boats fill the harbour
fish more plentiful in nets
meadows adorned with haystacks,

Woodbine permeates each hedge
emitting earth's sweetest scent,
eternal summer of you.

Bainne Géar

Na focail lácha a d'éalaigh
as a béal binn, stop
siad áit éigin eadrainn

chuir siad feisteas uafáis orthu féin
fiacla fada ina mbéil a d'fhéadfadh
craiceann is feoil a stróiceadh

clócaí dorcha thar a nguaillí
gúnaí dubha, aghaidheanna gan súile
gan bheola, gan cumas acu gáire

a dhéanamh, lámha críonna
le méara fada liatha
lámha le sceana in airde

an méid sin crúb ag na focail
iad thar chomhaireamh -
bainne géar ina gcíocha.

Earth ¦ Dúlra

Teagasc

Shíl mé riamh go raibh dath glas ar fhéar
is an ghrian in airde.

Nuair a d'iarr sé orm buí a chur ar mo scuab
chomh maith le glas agus donn chun féar

a phéinteáil isteach níor thuig mé, níor aontaigh
mé leis ach rinne mé amhlaidh.

Inniu féachaim amach an fhuinneog
agus feicim ribí buí i nglas an fhéir

paistí donna in áiteanna nár fhás aon ní.
Inniu tuigim dó den chéad uair riamh.

Winter in Our Garden

I want to eat the crispness of winter;
russet leaves on barbeque.
Sweeping the remnants of berries on decking
into the compost bin, sea shells

on the paving whisper June's name.
Porous Moycullen stone
fossilised around flowerbeds
views the last of this year's wild rose

trying to stay alive. Unused buckets
brim with water, foliage swims like lillies
on a pseudo-Roman bird bath.
Bare trees direct sunlight, not knowing which shrubs

will survive another season.
Adopted wild cat frolicking with her kittens
that are now indistinguishable
from their parents. Some shinny up a dwarfed Yew

which marked our first winter together.
I wonder that it has not turned briar.
Birds still tweet and caw amidst concrete noise,
worms slither beneath dead leaves, spiders weave webs.

Fáinleoga

Fáinleoga ar líne teileafóin
mar a bheadh rian scuaibe
de phéint liath ann ó mhórealaíontóir,

iad ag feitheamh don turas ó dheas
faoi scáth a máistir atá díreach tar éis
an ghrian a tharraingt isteach.

Ag dul soir
airím gaoth fhuar,
easpa muiníne mar reoiteoga ionam.

Éiríonn an lá níos gile.

PORTAL

Winter Atlantic water making small white birds of itself
as it strolls towards the shore in a piecemeal fashion.
I thought the whites alive at first,
wondered where this colony hailed from,
they stretched from Murisk Head right across Clew Bay.

A streak on the pane places a flag
on the summit of the bump that rests
between two Nephins. Black wispy clouds
try to veil lumps of snowy sunshine
but fail to stop sea-mountain illumination.

Not even the most adept painter
could transfer such velvet shadows
and brown mountain light that warms my eyes;
the crushed multi-blue silk of the ocean,
pagan god emerging through cloud above Croagh Patrick,
gothic cattle revere grass,

hilly bramble-stitched right-of-ways,
walks to the strand, distant houses are pearls
strung at the feet of hills. Wagtail hopping
on the pavement outside taps out hunger.
Bright and dark cloud worlds collide,
a rainbow forms beneath them;

orange aflame, red edging,
yellow sandwiched between green and indigo,
no extending arc, just bare essentials. Not of this world.
I want to search for a forgotten people where the rainbow
sinks into the foothills. As I lift my eyes from the page

I notice all has disappeared, even the clouds.
Ancient rocks that wouldn't be moved are whispering
something to its place of sacrifice on the mountain,
breeze carries secrets into every curve of the bay.
Here the elements are the only gods.

EOLAÍ ÓG

Glóthach ghlas
i ngéibheann i bpróca,
athrú suntasach ag teacht ar an m*blob,*
bobailín le heireaball, cosa cúil,
cosa tosaigh, gan eireaball.

Cromann páiste óg síos
ag iarraidh greim a fháil ar an bhfrog
ach é imithe uaidh arís.
Ní hamhlaidh do na torbáin
ag snámh fós sa bpróca nó i bpoll,

ag fanacht ar an uair
a bheidh sé in am dóibh
an t-uisce a fhágáil
agus de chumas acu léim
ó lámha fiosracha an eolaí óig.

ANOTHER FAMILY

I look out at the family of cats, mother and five sucklings,
scampering around on my wooden decking.
They tell us not to feed strays,
my heart went out to her after she lost last winter's litter

to inclemency and hunger. Slipped out the odd saucer
of milk early summer when I saw her swollen body.
Couldn't bear to witness her dead carried to my door
a second time. One morning when going to the clothes line

I startled as I walked out the back, felt something alive
on the top of the turf barrel. Standing at a safe distance
I glanced, moving balls of fur and mammy cat.
She hissed, respectful of her territory on my turf I withdrew

to the garments that were strung across the back yard,
felt I had saved a family. Myself and my young watched
the progress of the furry balls that eventually unwound
to form miniature caricatures of their mother;

ones of different colour taking after the other side.
Awed at the way x's and y's blend shades of coat.
Perhaps they were wild but they gave us endless pleasure
to watch them play-scrape at and scamper up the dwarf

yew in the centre of the garden, heard claws sharpen.
When I opened the back door its noise made them
skedaddle to their new nest behind the wood pile.
Weeks passed, their capers became fewer and fewer

until there was barely a trace. I vainly stared
out the window, realising they had found a different alley
in which to serve apprenticeship.
Very few months later a cat doing reconnaissance

of last year's labour ward. Now a new family of five squat
on my turf, even more playful than their older siblings,
they rugby-huddle under the garden table during showers,
one big pouf of soft fur.

Aréir chuir an oíche a feisteas is áille uirthi,
gealach mhór bhuí,
ní raibh mé ag tabhairt aire don bhóthar
is mé ag tiomáint,
fiú ag dul thar choirnéal

níor éirigh liom gan féachaint uirthi.
Ní fhéadfá í a shárú, spéir dhorcha,
ag éirí níos dorcha fós,
gealach ag éirí níos gile
mar a bheadh lampa nua ann.

Go tobann tháinig na réaltaí amach.
Ón uair a chuala mé go raibh cuid acu
níos mó agus níos teo ná an ghrian féin
is iomaí sracfhéachaint a fuair siad uaim,
cuid acu ag pléascadh, cuid eile ag titim

agus ní réaltaí cuid áirithe eile ach pláinéid!
Bhí cuma orthu gur léim siad amach
ó shaol draíochta éigin,
níor fheil a n-áilleacht don domhan seo.

Athraithe

Síol ag fás
ag forbairt a phearsantachta,
géaga ag luascadh,
sásta,
ag dul i dtaithí ar an saol
de réir a chéile,
síol gruama, uaireanta.

Síol i measc síolta,
cosúil nó éagsúil
ceapann síol óg
go bhfuil sé níos fearr
a bheith éagsúil,
rud nach fíor, taithí,
athraíonn an síol beagáinín.

Síol ag iarraidh a shíolta
a chur is a scaipeadh,
cuid acu fiáin, cuid séimh.
Saol an tsíl athraithe go mór,
tuilleadh taithí. Faoi dheireadh
tuigeann síol seansíolta.
Síol aibí.

LUXURIES

Driving on Docks Road
one coal-yard afternoon,
grit and grime was airborne,

the interior of the car smelt
of burnt diesel,
multi-carbon monoxides

mingled in my lungs.
Just past where all the boats
are arrayed and anchored,

past emissions of tipper trucks
accepting luxuries, past padlocked gates
that bar human shapes,

I saw a pair of swans
flying low over water,
a sudden palpitation of hope.

Sea Breakfast

Looking up the coast towards Mulranny
from the height of Lecanvey
November morning sunlight heats Clew Bay.

Some of the small Islands look like
they are dropped scones set to cook
in winter's hearth. A large yacht is filling

in a tiny-island sandwich.
I would have loved to have painted the water,
Titanium White, little splash of Aquamarine on my brush,

long even strokes, horizon line fading, blending with sky,
unsurpassable diet,
boiled egg and black pepper on the table,

satisfaction complete.

Moon Song

Massive orange gold moon that made me think
the world was ending the night I spied it
outside the front door of our house, terrorised me.
Later representations that had a witch cycling past
on a broomstick did nothing to quell my fears.

When I see it now, we exchange pleasantries,
harvest moon, glowing the colour of corn or ripe fruit.
Wishy-washy winter moon doing a striptease in the sky,
wafting cloud veils in front of its face, disappearing
momentarily then re-emerging in all its naked glory.

Summer moon that thinks it's the sun, wants people
to be fooled when they search the bright evening sky
until the round ball drops; there can't be two suns!
Hold on a minute, which one is the impostor?
Wouldn't you think one would have the decency

to absent itself when it wasn't needed?
Watch them vie for brightest light in the heavens,
subverting time, night, romance.
"How about a sunlit walk love?" doesn't have the same
ring to it. Grow moon of spring is the favourite son

of any constellation. It lights bulbs of snowdrops and crocus
that hibernate in cold earth. As tiny flowers grow
the moon trumpets, everything follows suit
as the news catches every breeze and warms it.

Walk On Old Head

A girl on horseback takes the coast road
ignores all signs of rock angling,
our course takes us to Old Head beach.

Walking the strand a white shape in the water
is an unusual bird made entirely from plastic.
A black, what looks like duck,

with snow breast feathers bobs alongside
the would be swan. I trace shapes in sand,
someone appears to have dragged a branch

all the way down to the sea. On closer inspection,
tiny rivulets of stream flow through the grain,
looking up, a grass cliff with gurgling spring.

A foamy surf shoots its cannon at our feet.
I pick up a scallop shell as large as an ashtray.
Always on the look out for pearls

but normally only intercept crab claws
or lobster body parts.
Our thirst quenched in Derrylahan.

Pink clot.
Green backdrop.
Yellow thumbs.
Purple throat.

Thorny heart held aloft,
several dangling limbs.
All neatly arranged
on a lily shroud.

Reflection

On mirror water
Lir's children uptail,
nosedown, looking for roots.
In the background

the cragged leftovers
of a crannóg
bears upright shoots
of no circumference.

I feel a feather-gaze,
meeting it I see
a thousand rings
in the eyes of a swan.

TWINS

You wouldn't believe it –
thirty yards before lunch,
not another break
until nearly eight
when you could see the sun
cast a shadow
on Old Brown's Bog.

Mark me this,
not a sod went to waste,
unlike what was machine-cut.
Some men with a *sleán*
those twins,
the last time I saw them -
knee-high to a grasshopper.

Down at the shore, birds
blinded by the night
flew in my face, Hitchcock-like.

They didn't look like sea birds,
land-frail the whispering waves scared them.
Across the bay lights gleamed,

birds frightened of the dark shore sky
finally retreated, beckoned
by some invisible signal.

Alone on the beach
I listened
to the secrets of water.

Down at the Harbour

The outline of the Aran Islands
pops above the horizon
old car tyres are portholes
on the harbour wall

gas barrels stacked
telegraph poles come
to an abrupt halt
red car draws trailer

up from the shore
and fades away home
a horse strides its stone perimeter
colourful boats that bob like corks

are attached to the harbour wall
two upturned currachs are sleeping
seaweed scattered over stone and sand,
another layer of sea debris,

grey haired man forks seaweed
into a car trailer
bird drinks from drying stream below
and disappears under the Romanesque arch

of the bridge. White sandy coastline ebbs away.
two gulls, mid-flight, flirt outrageously.

When the mountain cried
its tears were rivers
a cold hearted sister sprung glaciers

which could not outflow
the volumes of tears
that meandered as they matured

shedding the odd oxbow lake
in old age
that it cast aside like loneliness

guided by the birds of the moon
in its infirmity it moved slowly
only to converge with offspring

where the sea's petticoat skirts the shore.

Swans, herons, robins
baby birds in nests
their pink featherless flesh
wide open beaks

morning's dawn symphony
all used to conjure beauty
now as I scan the newspapers
searching for any mention

of H5NI anywhere
in the environs of Ireland
chicken burgers, breasts,
drumsticks, crispy duck,

Christmas fowl
all exiled from the menu.
Recently everywhere
resounds with birdsong

but the only image
that springs to mind
is a deadly viral strain,
the power to annihilate humankind.

The café at Old Head remains closed
but bodies throng the sands,
divers line up to jump off the harbour wall in turn,
sun has lightened winter's heavy oil-colours to pastels,

In a battered old van a pension-aged English couple
hawk teas and ice-creams,
jelly babies in rows of delight.
Beach-tents stand erect,

umbrellas pierce the sand,
towels allsorts, a mix of colours,
skin turns different shades of red
vitamin of laughter pervades.

Journey ¦ Aistear

I keep your image among poems
that recall being in your company
not ones penned in adoration

poems that were read
when sitting next to you at dinner,
you filled my glass.

Trees, heather, bog all roll by
towards you in first class carriage.
Barley yellowed in post summer heat

hails harvest. My lines reach
for the other side of the page,
never again will I sit next to you at dinner.

Ar phríomhbhóthar Chamden
díoltar púicíní draíochta,
piocann fear déirce
bun toitín suas ón gcosán
is caitheann sé é.

Fiche punt ar naoi n-unsa
de phúicíní draíochta ón gColóim
nó ón nGuine Mheánchriosach.
Dath rastaiféarach ar luaithreadán,
boscaí beaga nó píopa do raithneach,

rudaí a bhíonn ag teastáil
ó dhaoine nach bhfuil
chomh sean liom féin,
feicim clóca m'óige
thíos fúm ar an mbóthar.

Ardaíonn an ghaoth,
séidtear duilleoga im éadan,
ní féidir mo shlí abhaile
a aimsiú tríd an smionagar.

Bleeding Sunset

Sun bleeds over Galway Bay
light scattering

it is pink to beyond the ocean
I think it bleeds for me.

It knows the bruises that map
my thighs, extending to my knees.

Night doesn't require camouflage.
Often what is too disguised

becomes glaring
thankfully my face escaped tonight.

Saoire

Sa chuan seo tá caiple bána
ag teacht isteach
dath donnairgid ar an trá,

triúr éagsúla
ag siúl ar an ngaineamh.
osclófar an linn snámha

arís do shaoire na Cásca
i gceann sé mhí, muid ag siúl
ar na carraigeacha

an ghrian ag iarraidh teacht tríd
gan dóthain airgid agam
triall ar an Spáinn

ach bainimid sult
as ár seachtain i dTír Chonaill
cois trá.

Waiting

He peered through the beer coloured curtains
Flaherty's will see it first
not wanting to be the odd proprietor out
the only one found with his door open

across the road her head swivelled back and forth
his cue, her open door.
He danced from window to tap and back
in case he'd miss a customer.

It was a doctor you know, hardly sixty
the procession so big
it almost blocked the whole street
Don't close the door yet

Keep an eye on your one across the road
You never know the day nor the hour.

Beiriste

A céile díreach curtha
Fiche bliain tar éis a máthar
Breis is deich mbliana tar éis dearthár léi
cúpla mí tar éis a deirféar.

Ise chomh haclaí, cliste,
Níor loit tobac ná alcól riamh a corp,
ba mhinic a dúirt sí nach mbíonn éinne ag súil
lena mbás féin, nach mbíonn siad ag díriú ar an mbás.

Níor iarr sí ach an bóthar a thrasnú
cluiche beiriste ag fanacht uirthi
ba bheag nach raibh sí lena céile arís an oíche sin.

Í ar leaba an bháis ar feadh na míosa
muid timpeall uirthi,
iontas ar chuile dhuine nuair a d'éirigh sí arís.

Millennium spread with enough adipose
to carpet the Sahara, leftovers to make curtains
and tie-backs with pelmets to match

highway between the ears has melted
to a narrow track of a humped back bridge, iced over.
Foresight now hindsight with fog lights

motor movements in the slow lane
everything mid medium or average
except when referring to waistline

which is outsize. Nothing rare or unusual
unless referring to ribs or methods of cooking.
Difficult phenomena to explain

I thought this was the age of experience, maturity, reason.

Doldrums in a Monaghan Town

Between the drumlins and dolmens,
clay headed with stony toes
I statue my progression
catapult a career back ten years

In these spiralling times
rock toes unable to ascend –
town on the rise –
between the drumlins and dolmens

I fold. Good intentions accordioned
to former inglorious stagnation.
I twin with this hilltop town that died
the year the border sneaked in,

its economy under guerrilla attack
wounds wrapped in American band aids.

Soft shapes flow
nightgowned and slippered
breeze through doors and arches

pink, blue, navy hands out,
feet follow the waves.
Greetings to all fellow inmates

difficult to differentiate between
staff and patients.
I peep out of the corner of my pillow

and see all the startlings
sink deeper into the bed board
and dream of my release.

House full of uncompleted things;
cards that were never posted,
dreams are cobwebs lurking in corners,
over bedsteads, inside windows,
escape impeded.

Forsaken photos, dust covered films,
cassettes ignored, music never played.
No thump of radio or breaking air waves
of news, no buzz of turning pages
or ink dribbling coherently on leaves.

But the light of spring still sneaks in.

I rith Aifreann na Marbh
ní raibh le cloisteáil
ach gáire gasúir
ón scoil bhéal dorais.

Tháinig sórt náire orm
is mé ag bun an tséipéil,
náire orm gurbh fhéidir
gáire a dhéanamh

is tú ag fulaingt. Thug mé
faoi deara go raibh ciorcal
fulaingthe thart ort,
thart ar do ghruaig fhionn chatach.

D'fhéach mé arís ar d'éadan,
cuma an pháiste ort féin.
Leath an spraoi ón mbunscoil,
ní fhéadfá srian a chur ar scléip,

fiú nuair a bhíodh Mac Dé id bhéal.
Ní raibh sé chomh fada ó shin
ó bhí tú féin id naíonán,
chomh cosúil lena chéile tú féin

agus an té in aice leat sa chónra,
a bhíodh lán le spraoi an tsaoil.
Smaoinigh mé ar eaglaisí éagsúla
a bhíonn suite gar do scoileanna,

an fhadhb chéanna ag gach sochraid
ach amháin i lár an tsamhraidh.
Le déanaí táim cleachtach ar adhlacthaí.
Líonadh an séipéal le Gaeilge,

an urnaí is binne a chualathas riamh.

Up The Walls in Dubrovnik

The woman who charged me fifteen Kuna for bottled water
while I walked on the walls of the city of Dubrovnik
has a husband in a wheelchair
who would argue with the spokes of his wheels.

Their argument is so heated they can't hear the Italian
tourists gasping for lollies. How can they fight,
sun beating down on the Adriatic,
its water laps the rocks below. Is it not their castle?

As I follow the margin of the fortress the apartments on the
left have washing hanging on the balconies, smell the surf!
Gas or no gas? the old woman asked before handing me
the water. No gas, her husband blows quite enough of that.

I picture myself on one of my non-existent maps of Europe,
a glowing dot on the coast of Croatia. Inside the city walls
there are several catholic churches and only one mosque.
Ignorant of the politics of the people, I feel their suffering.

How many Balkan crises did this unhappy couple endure?
Outside the walls there is a chart; triangles for direct hits on
roof tops, circles for when they met their target
on the pavement, pink for buildings gutted by fire,

pink triangles for roofs set ablaze, dots mark artillery holes.
On the other side of the old city the pulse of boats
jettying tourists to an island on the bay soothes besieged
thoughts. Beside me an English couple in superior voice

talk about the walls of Chester. A pigeon pooh poohs,
then flies off. Downwind from the tourists, their cigarette
smoke is in my line of fire. I baulk at the pollution
of fresh sea air. My writing is not a conversation piece

but it whips the blues away. Where better to bask than
overlooking red rooftops to my left, white rock and ocean
to my right? Islands are the sea's vermillion. I pass
a Muslim couple with two kids doing the wall walk.

Anytime they are within earshot of other tourists
they switch from Arabic to English.
The old man in the wheelchair starts shouting again.
His wife shouts back. I feel such a mono-linguist

when I hear others around me speak Italian, German,
and French. The old couple's daughter, who flogs her past
in pastel and ink against the outside of the shop wall,
joins the argument. A seagull glides overhead, bells,

in tiers like a wedding cake, calls the believers.
Through an ancient porthole I see yachts on the jetty below,
turrets every few steps, some mosque-like,
some medievalesque. Later at lunch on the cobbles below,

my senses were assailed by two Americans
at a neighbouring table; they tested the meaning
of tolerance. Ignorance is bliss for dessert, the worst
of understanding English in foreign parts.

A friendly Croatian waiter greeted me in Gaelic
with a *blas* that would make an islander blush. I see red
stones on the beach the same colour as rooftops
and wonder is this the first sighting of the terracotta

pebble? At the gate of this great city, oranges, bursting out
of their skin, cling to trees, some drop and split
like conkers, over-ripe fruit. The staff in the hotel,
moustached to a man, are more like curators of a mosque

than waiters. What do they think of a woman
travelling alone? I arrange pebbles on my dressing table;
some terracotta, others as white as coconut flesh.
Across the road from my accommodation

the Adriatic ripples like a lake in the morning sun.
Old men turn their wooden boats upside-down,
a common phenomenon, a faint x in the sky
where two plane paths crossed. Three yachts

with their sails up are folded white handkerchiefs,
an old man with trousers to his knees sketches a girl lying
on towels at the edge of the beach,
then he exclaims in disgust at his drawee.

Swimmer's arms come up for air in turn, handkerchiefs
have subdivided many more times, and their troop
lines the horizon. Swimmer disappears from view,
my eyes search the water to no avail,

stone surface is warm on my spine. Swimmer re-appears,
brown arms straight ahead, yachts race towards rocks.
I feel like telling the swimmer to come in before they kill
themselves, then I realise I don't know my own capabilities

not to mind theirs. Air smells of the sweet mixture of sea
and sun cream. Aqua-bliss. Seven windsurfers are seven
circling white sharks; two more upright fins ascend down
the rocky hill, though I know that they really emerged

from the hidden cove in time to beat the noon tide.
I dip my feet into the bath of the Adriatic;
a distant yellow speedboat is the odd man out,
schoolboys play soccer on offshore concrete,

seabirds caw like crows. I dream that an incoming boat
is my own white knight that won't leave me sitting here
waiting for the sun. The ocean is infinitely more interesting
than the people on it. Impostors! What intrigues

do they cast upon the shore? The day, in the shape
of an hour glass, slowly the sand trickles, sun blazing
its reflection. A local is single-handedly forming a pebble
beach of his own with barrowfuls of washed stone,

smooth from the attentions of the sea. The soothing sound
of the ocean's wash erases a recent nightmare, my hands
on the cool rock, I feel grounded. Most of the males here
want to battle the sea with boats or boards

or hook and sinker. Girls soak sedentary rays.
Further along the bay the people in the Fashion Cafe near
the Kumar don't serve those with unshaved legs,
who only drink bottled water and don't smoke.

It's the only joint in Dubrovnik where water is cheaper
than beer; everyone is Italian, white skin and blacked out
glasses. Taking a bus to Mostar from the Pearl of the
Adriatic was like re-entering a past war that you thought

was already won. Its streets were debris. At the Turkish
house we took off shoes, Imam's prayer echoed through
the bazaar, it sounded like a Conamara lament. The city
looked as if its inhabitants tried to out church one another,

peace having been foisted upon them, the more mosques
the Muslims built, the higher the Croats went
with their catholic steeples. The outlying Turkish town
has only sixteen families, each pawn their wares. En route

we overlooked Little California with its neat rows
and squares of olives and tangerines, vines everywhere.
A five kilometre wall midway up a mountain reminded
the guide of the Great Wall of China, it defied

fifteenth-century Venetians. Anyone was better
than the Venetians, the guide said. I wondered about this
when I heard that they sold a strip of coastline to the Turks.
It wasn't long before the Ottomans became the sick man

of Europe but Islam lives in the narrow cobbled streets
of Mostar's eastside and within Dubrovnik's city walls.
I gazed out the bus window again
at the vermillion of islands along Croatia's coast.

Triúr a chuir préamhacha síos inár bhfód,
shaibhrigh siad ár n-ithir,
ba mhinic a bhlaiseamar a sáibhirne;
puimpcín, cluiche peile, lámha cúnta.

Fásra samhraidh faoi bhláth,
spéir gan scamall, talamh cheal fearthainne le fada,
féar á bhaint, páistí ag treabhadh scathán an locha,
lena ngéaga, ainmhí ina luí faoin ngrian.

Th'éis lá mar seo a chnag ár dTiarna ar a ndoirse.
Cé nach raibh siad le chéile
fuaireamar ár seacht mbás
leis na scéaltaí a chloisteáil.

An bhféadfadh sé a bheith ina shamhradh a thuilleadh?
Ag gach cluiche peile smaoinímid ar Mhaitiú,
i lámha Dé atá sé ó thús mhí Iúil seo caite.
Lasann a réaltóg an spéir gach oíche.

Tá Dara fós linn sna crainn a chuir sé, sna bláthanna
a bhronn sé, sna beithígh a leigheas sé,
sna fir is na mná ar chabhraigh sé leo,
sna gasúir áille a d'fág sé anseo.

Má bhuailtear bob ar éinne ar an mbealach
go hEanach Cuain ní fhéadfaí an milleán a chur ar Bhrian.
Ní raibh sé ach ag teacht chun fómhair,
Deora mar dhuilleoga ag titim.

Is fada a bheas trácht,
i gcéin agus i gcóngar,
ar an triúr cairde a cailleadh
i rith an tsamhraidh dhá mhíle is a ceathair.

I measc a ndaoine maireann siad.

Train

Sitting at opposite ends
We both looked at the castle
At the boats on the river
At our watches when those alongside
Wouldn't cease talking.

Spanish Holiday

Children inside plastic life harness
were colourful flying fish suspended in sunshine,

next deckchair down a couple speaking Gaelic,
many tattoos sported varying degrees of swimness,

chunky novels being read,
white, red, bronze, tan; some colours not turning.

The sun fooled everyone and sent a few drops of moisture
earthwards. Now we worship more ardently than before.

My kingdom for an ice cream
or a long cool drink, beer, wine, cigarettes go cheap.

Everyone's touting for business; all soaps shown nightly,
Sky Sports v GAA Championship, Full English breakfast,

Irish Stew, Jolly Pirate, Lucky Leprechaun. Wait until the
last day to court the sun. It spits down instead of splitting

the stones. They say it hasn't rained since February,
it's now the close of June, even the palm's lower branches,

brown, bow in thanks to the God of rain.

"*Tempus Fugit* in Fitzgeralds"
dongs the grandfather clock with a yellow wrinkled face,

a press of a bell calls the old man, his art-deco eyes,
Persian-rug feet notice my mother-of-pearl hands

hoping to encircle amber wrists, crystal neck
and matching lobes with one offs from his hotel window

and lobby case. From my handbag a Mastercard
takes flight. I listen to yarns of his wandering daughter

who collects and sells, to tales of an old customer
who, like me, transfixes on the gaudy ware,

later I searched the beach for angel seats.

September evening in Lecanvey
eyes skimming the quiet Atlantic,
from the rock where I sit
the part of Clare Island in view

and the jutting out piece of coast past Mulrany
are the Gates of Hades.
Nephin is blowing puffs of smoke skywards,
as the clock winds towards twilight

the mountains put on a light blue negligée
and appear distant. A lone sailor is half an inch
away from the horizon. Earlier in the day the
hump of Clare Island reminded me of a whale

emerging from the ocean but in the dim dusk light,
from my vantage point, it is clearly a snail
after abandoning its shell, making a bee line for a morsel
of food within easy reach. The sharp edged stone

at the bottom of the garden is the Pillar of Hercules,
when I stood at the real thing I didn't gaze
on a sight more beautiful that this island speckled bay.
Behind the house *Crúch Phádraig* stands

at over seven hundred feet. Patrick's house blocks out
Mecca to the East. No Imam near to hand. According to
a local anecdote when Imam comes to call on the Hal Al
meat plant everything is strictly by the Koran,

different story when he turns to face east,
his back to their westerly ways.

A Fresh Letter to Billy Collins or 'Wet and Wild'

Dear Bill,
indeed humbled to receive your mail,
kindness itself to take a break
from your laureatness to communicate
with an ardent admirer
this side of the Atlantic.

I confess to regular imaginary sex
with your poetryness.
How to categorise my sin ...?
Not adultery, bigotry or plagiarism ...
Unsure if you are aware that this
Irish lust, subliminal in the most part,

has a range of two thousand miles plus.
You transport me to 'Old Irish' lectures,
for you the stag bellows ninth century,
for me, "*wet and wild are the winds tonight,*
they toss the tresses of the sea to white,
on a night like this I take my ease,

fierce Norsemen only course the quiet seas".
The class knells in my head,
a student on a J1, I flew to Wildwood,
behind bars of a cosmetic counter
in the Boardwalk Mall I fingered eye pencils,
lipstick, shadows, all '*Wet 'n Wild*',

during quiet moments transcribed
Old Irish verse on odd bits of cardboard,
anything to preserve what little sanity left.
I dream of you; wallpaper, classical mice,
nice cultural holidays, but in reality
all I want is for you to present yourself
during the Galway races,

Colette.

Gach duine ag féachaint ar an gcluiche
teach tábhairne galánta
deisceart Bhéal Feirste
deireadh na hoíche

thairg tú suíochán do bhean
d'iarr do bhuachaill ort
suí ar a ghlúine
thoiligh tú

níor thug tú faoi deara
nach bhfuil áit don duine aerach
sa phróiseas síochána
iad neamhchompordach

led leithéid
sa bharda *gerrymander*áilte seo.
Chiceáil siad thú
is tú thíos

briseadh do rúitíní,
scoilteadh do chloigeann
gan cumas agat siúl
ach d'eitil do spiorad in airde.

Islam doesn't do *Barbie*
the world's best loved doll,
brown-eyed *Fulla*

is her Muslim counterpart,
Fulla's breasts are smaller,
body covered in a black *abaya*

or robe and matching scarf,
she has a *Barbie*-pink
felt prayer mat.

Some brand the doll
an Islamic strategy,
they hope the *Fulla* craze

doesn't snowball.
Fulla vies with *Barbie,*
society divides,

with prayer mat or without,
listen children,
to lesson one in discord.

PROPAGANDA

Stalking the room like something trapped
waiting to break free or be released,

to do, teach, wish each piece of literature
might live, each forced essay fade

into the pseudo-utopia where they were created
only to loiter on the periphery of unseasoned minds.

Dictated lies, learned untruths
someone else's knowledge

verbatim from books or study splints
of hope. Their focus shows the pain

of night before cram, mine, the rush
of papers to ready, to set.

How different is this education from the Fascist
states of the thirties or Stalinist Russia?

Different Colours

Across the city to the other side
tripped over wire crossing the peace line,

people, pavements, bunting, flags
wore different colours

but I only noticed your eyes
softness of hair

slimness of fingers
interesting words that rose above others

either side of the sectarian divide
the need for barriers subsided.

I knew what it meant to be a political refugee
when I saw him take the call that said that his brother
had been buried for three days, they couldn't reach him
but even if they had …

Four years prior to this he missed his mother's funeral.
It was Sunday, his head lowered as he read *The Observer*,
fingers across his brow, he didn't look up. Tea drops
stained the table cloth, outside the ocean drank

the evening sun and smacked its red lips.
Driving home past the house where my mother lived,
past the houses of my brothers, past my sister's house
I noticed the moon was only a shadow of its former self.

Hijab: Mhothaigh mé go raibh mé cheal éadaigh
Nuair a d'fhéach sé orm, ar mo chorp. B'fhéidir
Nach ar mo chorp ar chor ar bith a bhí sé ag
Féachaint ach ar rud éigin eile a bhí ag snámh idir
Mé agus é féin. Bhraitheas a shúile ag baint mo
Chuid éadaigh díom, diaidh ar ndiaidh go dtí
Nach raibh mé ag caitheamh rud ar bith ach éadan
Chomh dearg le sú talún. Tabhair dom Hijab.

Khimar: Sa leaba, níos déanaí sa tráthnóna,
Pluid á tarraingt thart orm, ag clúdach gach
Rud suas go dtí mo smig, mé cromtha faoi
Philiúr, lámha thar mo cheann, ní fhéadfainn
dada a chloisteáil, mo shúile dúnta, ag smaoineamh
air. Ach cé hé féin? Cén chaoi a bhfuil a fhios agam
nach dúnmharfóir é? Níl a fhios agam rud ar bith faoi.
Léigh mé a gháire, a shúile. Chreid mé.
Uaireanta ní bhíonn uainn ach Khimar.

Niqab: Nuair a bhíos ag taisteal go Sasana
D'athraigh chuile shórt nuair a chonaic
Mé í sa scuaine linn. Roimhe sin bhíos cinnte
Nach raibh oiread is braon amháin den chiníochas
Ag rith tríom, ach, nuair a fheicim arís í
Braithim an faitíos a bhain na cosa díom.
Í gléasta i ndubh, gan le feiceáil ach a súile.
B'shin go gairid tar éis 9/11. Bhíos ag guí
Nach mbeadh sí ar aon eitleán linne.

A feisteas a chuir ar mo mhíshuaimhneas mé
Ach bhí sí linn don turas. Léim na rudaí a dúirt
Sí sa nuachtán im aigne; cearta an duine, fuascailt
Creidimh, fuascailt na mban, go mbeadh siad níos
Gaire do Dhia de bharr an feisteas a bheith orthu.
Ní fheadar. Niqab.

Burqa: D'fhéadfá go leor málaí *a/wear* a chur faoi,
D'fhéadfá siopa beag a chur faoi. An laitís sin ag
Cur a n-éadan faoi cheilt ag insint dúinn nach bhfuil
Cearta ar bith ag an té atá taobh thiar di. Tuige
go bhfuil mná fós á chaitheamh? Nár cuireadh deireadh
leis an Taliban? Níl deireadh leis an scrios, áfach.
Níl deireadh le daoine á gcur faoi chois. Déarfainn
Go bhfuil dóthain ban ag iarraidh an *Burqa* a chaitheamh
Ar leataobh ach céard a cheapann na fir? An mbeadh
Siadsan sásta ligint leo? Nach ceart go mbeadh cead
Ag mná oideachas a fháil nó dul amach ag obair?

In áiteanna éagsúla níl cead ag mná titim i ngrá,
Cuireadh chun báis iad go dtiocfadh sé chun solais
Go raibh grá bán acu roimh phósadh. Ní bhíonn aon rogha
Ag na mná áirithe seo nuair a thagann sé chun cleamhnas
A dhéanamh ach an oiread. Roghnaíonn a gclann, na fir
Shinsearacha sa chlann. Ní bheadh sé béasach a gcuid
tuairimí a chur in iúl. Díoltar iad. Díoltar na mná seo go
minic Ionas go mbeadh oideachas ag na fir sa chlann.
An bhliain dhá mhíle is a cúig agus a leithéid fós ag tarlú.

NO CHANCE OF REPATRIATION

Gorse bushes are torches lit by summer,
unkempt grass in the centre of the track
strokes the underbelly of the car,
a gate or two yawns open,

no visible sign of Joyce's cottage,
not even a stone on the bog,
as if the turf swallowed it whole
eliminating any chance of repatriation.

The old yard has yielded a tennis court,
Firs have been supplanted. Laurels
haven't yet learned their rustle,
apples have grown smaller on trees,

pears crabbed. A henhouse empty of hens
adopts a stony faced stance and hides
behind the forced arch of witch-hazel.
Rose's garden is a ghost yielding nettles.

I imagine you casting out
from the harbour at Keel
or perhaps in a boat offshore
reeling them in.

Later, sea-hungry,
you light a fire on the beach
barbecue your catch
chase it with long cool draught.

Imagine music playing as you sit
peaceful waves and lullaby moon
imagine dancing around June's fire
summer passion tattooed on your skin

as the knowledge of Finn blistered on his.
Imagine it survived the same time span
I look out the window and exalt the moon
envious of the stars over the strand at Keel.

I tried to ignore:
the lone magpie on the bog road
dead blackbird outside my window
assembly of dark clouds
blunt pencil that wouldn't be sharpened
the stars misaligned
empty bottle of red wine

extinguished fire from your cigarette
song of your phone in the middle of the night
lack of eye contact
broken pane of stained glass
sugar granules scattered on the table
your cup of Conamara fishermen left untouched
the way you walked in front or behind.

I tried to remember:
our first kiss
your insistence that we meet
our journey to the mountain top
your hand in mine
the fever of your touch
long walks on a rocky beach

requests for reassurance
touching remarks
lying on the grass listening to jazz
taking shade under an oak
discussion of common friends

talk of the past
camera in your grasp

meals shared
conversations enveloped in your arms
introduction to your world
mutual fears
your witty charm.
The tide has reached the harbour wall,
now that you have put the night between us

it rains in the dark.

Memories | Cuimhní

Aonarán

Tigh Mhamó ní raibh éinne eile ann
chun calóga a ithe am bricfeasta,
bhíodh leite againn sa bhaile,
níor tógadh uaim an siúcra
ach mé gan chabhair ag ní na ngréithre,
plátaí a chur ar ais ar an drisiúr,
a bheith in iontas leis an gciteal leictreach
nó an *Baby Belling* a fheiceáil in úsáid.

Ní raibh duine ar bith eile ann
chun an t-urlár a scuabadh nó móin a fháil,
níor ghlan aon neach eile an sorn,
níor airigh siad an clog ag crith ó nóiméad
go nóiméad nó an ghaoth ag pleidhcíocht lasmuigh,
gan trácht ar úlla beaga a ghoid
is a chaitheamh amach arís tar éis an chéad ghreim.
Mé féin amháin a ghlaoigh Uncail ón ngort,

tháinig a mhadra gan nod ar bith,
mise a roinn cáca milis mar mhilseog againn
a threabh tríd an *Reader's Digest* a tháinig ó Mheiriceá,
cead agam breathú ar an teilifís san iarnóin,
a leithéid de *Carry On* !
Mé ag guí go dtiocfadh an chéad bhéile eile
go mbrisfí ciúnas urnaí mo mháthar móire,
Tigh Mhamó, mé gan chomhluadar.

Homage

In the past men doffed hats
took off caps when entering the house.
I remember our neighbour had a feather in his,
he would remove hat from head to hands

on his thrice daily visits,
"God bless the work",
it wouldn't be donned again
until he made his exit.

In church men were bare headed
women, scarfed or veiled,
amazed at the widows black net
and vestments, I'm sure I stared.

Sunday's best produced many exotic scenes,
birds, stripes, circular triangles
tied beneath chin. Communion trail
the only opportunity to ascertain

trends of a backwater town.

Ceathrú Gealaí

Cím mant id bhéal oscailte,
áit as ar thit fiacail amach.
Sular tharla sé ar chor ar bith
bhí tú thar a bheith buartha faoi,

Cuma leat má tharlaíonn
a leithéid gach uile lá.
Más riail nádúir féin é
Ní thiocfadh leat dul i ngleic leis.

Ós rud é gur thit sé amach
fad is a bhí tú ag breathnú
ar *Sponge Bob Square Pants*
ba bheag nár thug tú aon ní faoi deara.

Fén am a ndeachaigh tú a chodladh
bhí tú cleachtaithe le feadaíl nua.
Is tú faoi shuan,
scrúdaigh mé d'aghaidh

bun os cionn ar an adhairt,
leath meangadh ceathrú gealaí
ar do bhéal,
mhothaigh mé é im bhroinn.

Rain To The Rescue

Frayed fingertips free sods
from their heather clinch
bog wants to hold onto its coat,

secret drains and swallow holes
hidden minefields to capture
would-be thieves

natives know the geography.
Rain to the rescue
it moats the bog

sodden turf doesn't turn
we leave the hollows untouched
children throw mud balls

an in-law recounts tales
of growing flax
barbecue at intermission.

Ag rothaíocht go dtí páirc an fhéir,
aoi a bhí ionam, mála im ghlac;
ceapairí is buidéil tae.

Léimeas thar bhalla pháirc an tobair.
Ar m'fheiceáil dóibh cuireadh stop leis an obair.
Cocaí féir ann, aonarán i ndiaidh aonaráin

is iad bailithe thart orm idir óg is aosta.
Cuid acu níos óige ná mé ach bhí neart taithí
agam féin ar bhaint an fhéir.

The Fiddler Finn Celebrating the Coming of a Fourth Decade

i.m. Mickey Finn

He lay on the floor stroking his fiddle
after sliding down, back up against the wall,
I staggered in and stumbled a dance,
no chance of a singing violin
just "mind my fucking fiddle".

Later a tornado to the local
most of Taylor's turned to stare
I wavered over to the bar
still oozing with poitín punch.

You stuck your Connolly sticker
on the loo door, we smiled
as we trampled your plastic socialism
onto the toilet floor.

As for the rest my memory fails
flashes of an innocent barman called Bubbles
lugging me home, not quite out of choice,
he fended off the wolfish gropes en route.

TAR ÉIS AN CLOIGEANN A BHAINT DÁ DHEARTHÁIR

Thar dhroichéad Sheárlais
chuig an eaglais
inar luigh an naíonán is clúití ar bith.

Beag bídeach, déanta as ór,
gléasta i ngach sórt rúfaí,
aistríodh a chulaith chuile chúpla uair.

Chuaigh mé ar mo ghlúine os comhair a altóra.
Ba é mo ghuí ná go mbainfeadh sé an mhallacht díom
a cuireadh orm nuair a bhain mé an cloigeann

dá dheartháir a bhí ar mhatal mo mháthar
tríocha éigin bliain ó shin. Cheannaíos paidrín
is leathchúpla leis mar chúiteamh.

Milk and Briquettes, Twenty Eight
wakes at six for relief rounds
mother proud of his deftest hour.

Young Ming, not quiet Fifteen
wrung six kittens necks
fed them to the greyhounds.

Wee Denny Harney, Ninety Four
hung his dog twice
it still followed him home.

Eagle Eye, just a lad, Fifty Five
trespassed home Halloween night
the shot passed close to his left side.

Olann

Olann taobh thiar di
sa chathaoir mhór
gan deis aici bheith ag ligint scíthe.
Chniotáil sí geansaí
fad a bhí sí
ag breathnú ar an *Late Late*
seachtain *Today Tonight* do sciorta.

Gráin agam ar gheansaithe
a d'athchniotáil sí
mise taobh léi
is í ag stiúradh biorán
gan breathnú riamh ar phatrún.
Bhraith mé teas na holla
gan geansaí riamh a chur orm.

Fog, a morning bog blanket
frowns on the edge of suburbia
everything has an ashen hue

the grey-blue of winter dawn
although I saw a daffodil
with a hint of summer on its skin

just yesterday, the day we filled ourselves
with griddle and maple.
syrup that swam all the way from Canada,

a vast ice filled land my eldest computed,
children discuss what sacrifice for lent.
One vows to give up washing dishes

or perhaps chewing gum, which he hates,
youngest promises to fast from sweets,
definite case of curl mid forehead.

All pleased that the black tea days have dissipated.

Tú id chodladh
ceithre oráiste
suite taobh led chloigeann.

Dhiúltaigh tú do leaba féin,
isteach leat i nead do mháthar,
maidin áirithe is ainmhí fiáin í

ach leánn tú a glór
led phóg.
Ceithre shamhradh ó bhí tú
ag fás ina broinn.

Sceacha mar a bheadh coill dúinne
leath bealaigh idir barr an bhóithrín
agus cúl an tí, leagamar clocha an chlaí,

isteach linn gur shroicheamar croí
ár bpáirce imeartha. Ag rith tríd
na craobhacha fuara le linn an tsamhraidh,

ag déanamh bóithríní beaga lenár gcosa.
Muidne i bhfolach ó ghlaonna, ón obair.
Sméara bána na sceach, iad lán d'uisce,

bhí tú gafa nuair a mhothaigh tú sú
ag sileadh síos do dhroim nó faoi do chluas.
Tada againn a bhí déanta ag *Matel* nó *Fischer Price,*

faic ag teastáil uainn
chun an t-uasmhéid spraoi a bhaint amach
seachas ár gcosa, ár lámha agus ár gcroíthe.

Sa Scáthán

Nuair a fhéachaim sa scáthán
Feicim buachaill a cuireadh chuig an bpríomhoide,
captaen na foirne
a fuair cárta dearg ón réiteoir.
Deartháir do bheirt eile

a chuireann suim sa WWE freisin
cé go bhfuil siad níos óige
agus, níos minice ná a mhalairt,
faoi chois aige, go liteartha.
Duine a chaith mí ag obair ar thionscnamh ar an mBrasaíl

ach a rinne dearmad ar é a thabhairt isteach leis,
neamhní sa teist, cé go mbeadh níos mó eolais aige
ar an Amasóin ná éinne eile dá aois.
é ag siúl amach leis an gcailín is áille sa scoil
cé nach bhfuil a fhios aici go fóill,

i bhfad ró-*cool* sleamhain anuas an balastar
ach d'fhéadfadh sé fós "frig siar leat" a rá
os comhair daoine fásta.
nuair a fhéachaim sa scáthán
sin an té a fheicimse, ní mise!

Nuair a bhíodh féar mar phríomhábhar sa chomhrá;
an raibh sé réidh le baint nó nach raibh
bhíodh teas an tsamhraidh faoi lánseol.

Cuimhní agamsa ar theacht le chéile sa ghort
tuismitheoirí, páistí, comharsana, uncail nó beirt,
cuairteoirí ó Mheiriceá, réidh don obair.

Comrádachas, scéaltaí grinn,
obair dheacair, lámha tinne, dath na gréine,
léinte caite ar leataobh.

Turas nó dhó go dtí an tobar, uisce fuar,
laethanta fada inár luí ar thráithníní,
teacht le chéile an tsamhraidh.

An Cuairteoir ab Fhearr

Ar cuairt orainn gach samhradh
níor tháinig sé riamh gan a mhála mór
lán go cluasa le bréagáin is éadaí.

B'aoibhinn liom nuair a bhíodh sé linn mí Lúnasa,
aimsir mo bhreithlae. Thugadh sé an bréagán ab fhearr
dom, é tar éis scéal na hócáide a fháil ó mo mháthair mhór.

An rud is deireanaí ó *Matel* im ghlac, mé ar bís.
Tagann sé fós gach samhradh
cé go bhfuil mo mháthair mhór faoin bhfód le blianta.

Chomhcheangail

Sa bhothán taobh amuigh
leatheitlíonn na spréacha
leánn na píosaí miotail
atá go daingean sa bhís.

Ghoilleann na bladhmanna ar a shúile,
greim agama ar phíosa rud éigin
is é á dheisiú.
Casaim mo cheann sa treo eile

ó na lampróga geala.
Feicim an tslat ag scaipeadh stéige,
miotalnascadh, sos againn,
mé ag spraoi le tairní,

boscaí folmha,
smiongair ilíochta. Glaoite ar ais
chuig an mbinse,
obair amháin a chomhcheangail muid.

Éalú

D'éirigh grian na Cásca
mhothaigh mé ciontach
ag baint taitnimh as áilleacht an lae

agus daoine eile ag fulaingt
inár dtimpeall, ar fud na cruinne.
Ní bheadh orm dul rófhada ó bhaile.

Chuir deirfiúr liom tús le seó na Cásca
do na gasúir, uibheacha faoi cheilt
sa bhféar fada. Chíoraigh siad na claiseanna

is na sceacha á lorg.
Bhain sí taitneamh as an sonas a scríobh
ar na haghaidheanna beaga timpeall uirthi.

Gan aon bhrí eile leis an gCáisc
do na páistí óga seachas tóraíocht ar uibheacha,
ní cuimhin liom cén uair a d'éalaigh ár gcreideamh uainn.

The Renault van was red and battered
a cast off in '84 from the old Post Office
one Tuesday morning we went to market
and bought two bright pink-eyed piglets.

We squeezed them into the back of the Renault
up front I guarded the Moses-basket
from perils and smells of frightened *bonabh*s
that indiscriminately pissed and shat upon us.

At pig farming we were only novice
a pig sty accompanied our cottage
we aspired to husbandry of highest standards
the neighbouring travellers lent us a horse

which they tied out back to feed on our grass
it kept a watchful eye on the *bonabhs*
commiserated when *two legs* didn't give any feed,
their meal was two cauldrons of ground-down pig.

One cold November morning when money was scarce
two legs decided the piglet's fate
the bacon factory at Roscrea was the sentence
it found more use for bladders than the Romans.

We were sorry to part with Socrates and Palladius
or as we fondly called them Rashers and Sausages.
Each time I look at bacon since
I immediately think of my pork friends

that we sent to the guillotine
with heavy conscience.

A Belfast Belle
she'd give you a ring in your ear
bombarding you with gory stories
and gruesome tales

until you'd be ready to blow a fuse
at *the Europa is the most bombed*
hotel in Europe, you know.
A secret knitter from the Ormeau Road

she harboured a dream
of opening a haberdashery.
Open it next door to the Europa
I told her, balls of wool

ceiling to floor, tiles of charcoal
beneath ashen grey spools
counters clean as new pins
everything patterned and numbered

bells and moss, simple cable and diamonds
the problem would be getting insurance.

Border

In north county Monaghan
I feel the hound of Ulster
nip at my weak heel.

Wind whiffs of the blood
of battles lost
air of regret.

Hedgerows and tree
steel themselves, defend
desire to extend their roots

into the soil of the abducted counties.

CLONES, 1998

Was Wesley right
this *pleasant town*
finely situated on rising ground
in the midst of fruitful hills

and of men *mild and unassuming*
short hair combed sleek
behind their ears?
if so it must be said

two centuries after the date
they have lost the *sanctified look*
assumed English accent
if not their indulgence in whiskey punch

judgements of *fire and water*
they the *pillars of rock*
lakes of sulphur
stonily defy Anglo-Saxon impostors

no linen millstone around their necks.

Art | Ealaín

Seomra Ceoil

do Steve Cooney

Dhá phéire cos ar ardán
leath acu nocht
bróga dubha ag bualadh adhmaid
níl cosa an cheoil nite anocht

a scamhóga ag ardú is ag ísliú,
tháinig Steve ar *Shanks' mare*
an turas ar fad ón Astráil
chun ceol a chur inár saol.

Ag eitilt timpeall na háite seo
tá ceol na bhfocal, ceol na nguthanna
ceol an bhosca is an ghiotáir
ceol na sreang á bplancadh go teann

ceol na féile Imram.

FIRST IMPRESSIONS

Calf skin into the past,
an open door. Art,
exquisite in rectangular wood,
canvassed the walls.

Secret nooks held parchment
as delicate as autumn leaves
scrawled with quill.
Fingers of history on the table

reflected a lack of shallowness.
Floors reverberated with antiquity,
air held the silent tune of poetry.
I stretched out my hand and touched the past

between lines of black ink.
Watched by familiar eyes
I shrink in deference,
wonder if you are sketching the closing scene,

fleshing out a new tale,
revising history
or perhaps revisiting it.
I have turned the page.

Ba é an chéad uair a bhuaileamar le chéile,
is an uair dheireanach mar a tharla.
Nuair ba léir cé chomh lag is a bhí sí
chuaigh mé as mo bhealach
chun moladh a thabhairt di.

Iontas uirthi go raibh a hainm
ar eolas agam, gur léigh is gur labhair mé
an mhionteanga inar scríobh sí
agus iad léite fiú go raibh puinn suime agam
ina cuid véarsaíochta.

A lámh im lámh, níor chroith mé í
ar eagla go mbrisfinn cnámh,
mé ag déanamh iontais as filíocht ag teacht
ó chorp chomh críonna, cam le haois.
Saoithe níos clúití ná í

ag teacht is ag imeacht
ach inti amháin a bhí iomlán mo chuid spéise
go dtí gur ghlac duine dá lucht leanúna m'áit.
Inné reoigh a cuid focal ar a béal,
theip orthu dul chomh fada lena méara.

Hole

I pasted your philosophy on the door of my bedroom
like some hang photographs on their wall.

No stain to cover up, on my door was the fist hole
of my frustration, the size of a hemmed in teenager

full of twenty-first-century angst,
an unheard confession or a missed soccer match,

but you fit it quite nicely,
each four lines of your philosophy

a new chapter. Now I glance at my bedroom door
nothing visible but the shape of your intellect.

Banfhile

Bean álainn
gruaig fhionn
ag insint scéalta dúinn

faoin láir bhán:
bhain mé sult as a scéal,
a peann ar pár

as an solas a las
nuair a labhair sí linn
as na nithe a thug sí faoi deara

as an tuiscint a d'fhás
nach raibh aon ghá a mhíniú
as a focal scoir, a focail lácha.

Kiltimagh: In Sight of Raftery 2006

Between sun and sculpture
rare birds from the wetlands call their mates,
a blackbird with a juicy worm in his beak
doesn't need to ascend to the highest leaves

he perches on the lower branches of the Sycamore
this, the day of Summer.
Later John O'Connor will open doors
to a more earthly chorus.

Through the window I see a drum kit
and signs to enrol for summer school.
A day to lie on the grass
naked granite Adonis rests against a pillar.

Bandstand is umbrella for four upholstered chairs.
On the railway platform a bronzed conductor
checks his watch but this train
will never take off, finding you asleep

and drop you in Claremorris,
It will never depart from this stunning art.
Angel protects museum gable
anxious to ward off destructive hands.

Carriage full of hedgerow, blossoms,
is its own wilderness.
When the jazz band gets into their swing
We lie under a tree and take in the skyscape.